Dice Activities for Math

Engage • Enrich • Empower

Mary Saltus, Karen Moore, Diane Neison,
Marcia Fitzgerald and Chet Delani

Printed in the United States of America.

This book is printed on recycled paper.

Order Number 215295
ISBN 978-1-58324-277-3

J K L M N 17 16 15 14 13

395 Main Street
Rowley, MA 01969
www.didax.com

Contents

Introduction iv

Notes to Teachers............................v– vii

Meeting the NCTM Standards.......... viii

One-Die Activities 1–25

Objectives

- Recognize die dot patterns
- Recognize numerals 1, 2, 3, 4, 5, 6
- Sequence numerals 1, 2, 3, 4, 5, 6
- Record numerals 1, 2, 3, 4, 5, 6

Two-Dice Activities 27–41

Objectives

- Recognize numerals 1 through 12
- Recognize number patterns 1 through 12
- Record numerals 2 through 12
- Recognize odd and even numbers

Three-Dice Activities...................... 43–48

Objectives

- Recognize numerals 1 through 18
- Recognize number patterns 1 through 18
- Record numerals 3 through 18
- Recognize odd and even numbers

Half-Die Activities........................... 49–56

Objectives

- Conceptualize half of a number
- Find half of numbers 1 through 18
- Recognize a mixed number as half of an odd number
- Recognize that half of an even number results in a whole number
- Recognize that half of an odd number results in the fraction $\frac{1}{2}$ or a whole number and the fraction $\frac{1}{2}$
- Practice adding numbers mentally and then dividing by 2
- Develop a sense of numbers as whole and mixed numbers

Tens and Ones Activities 57–70

Objectives

- Practice combinations that equal 10
- Practice adding tens and ones
- Conceptualize sets of 10
- Add ten to numbers 1 through 18
- Recognize number patterns when adding ten to a number (unit numeral remains the same)
- Recognize number patterns when subtracting a number from a number ending in zero
- Develop a sense of number and number patterns 1 through 100

Tic-Tac-Toe Activities.................... 71–93

Objectives:

- Review number concepts developed through the graph and chart activities
- Practice computation
- Develop number sense
- Develop game strategy
- Develop communication and cooperation skills

Introduction

The activities in *Dice Activities for Math* were created by teachers in their classrooms over a period of 10 years. These time-tested activities have been proven to engage children, develop their mathematical thinking, and empower students' belief in their ability to do math.

The activities in this book focus on the NCTM content standard of number and operations. They also address the NCTM process standards of reasoning, representation, and communication.

The authors currently use dice activities as part of their curriculum to train elementary grade teachers in how to teach mathematics. The activities require only dice, a commonly available manipulative that is used in a variety of learning settings. Although these activities were created in classrooms, they are easily adapted to home schooling and by parents who wish to participate in the mathematics education of their children. They also provide a powerful opportunity for struggling math students to rethink mathematics from a multisensory approach.

Our work is continually expanding, and we welcome any suggestions for modifications to these activities that will lead to greater mathematical thinking on the part of our students.

—The authors of *Math of Course*,
www.mathofcourse.com

Notes to Teachers

The Activities

Dice Activities for Math is designed for teachers and parents to use with children in grades K–3. These engaging, challenging, and fun activities build number sense and generate a conceptual base for number facts. One of the inherent values of the activities is that children enjoy revisiting them and, in so doing, have an opportunity to practice number facts without tedious paper and pencil drill.

Dice Activities provides opportunities to:

- reinforce number patterns
- construct efficient counting strategies
- construct and interpret graphs
- manipulate numbers mentally
- understand how numbers work
- develop fluency with math addition and subtraction facts
- introduce place value
- verbalize math understanding
- expose students to math vocabulary
- develop game strategy

The activities are organized into six sections. The first three sections use one-die, two-dice, and three-dice graphs and charts for adding, subtracting, and doubling numbers. The fourth section presents variations of halving a quantity using graphs and charts. In the fifth section, children are exposed to the concepts of tens and ones. The sixth section introduces fun Tic-Tac-Toe activities for practicing math facts, developing reasoning skills, and experiencing the probability of specific occurrences in tossing dice.

The first graph and chart activities focus on number pattern recognition. In the One-Die Match Graph activity (page 4), the child tosses a die and matches the pattern on the die with the dot pattern on the graph. The dot patterns are arranged in numerical sequence. The child places a token above the dot pattern, creating a graph. In the Match the Die Pattern activity (page 5), the child tosses the die, finds the corresponding dot pattern on the chart, and places a token. The dot patterns on the chart are randomly placed and visually more challenging than the graph activity. The next activities are a graph and chart matching a dot pattern to a numeral.

Following the introduction of the counting activities, the dice activities become more abstract. If a child has yet to mentally conceptualize a number plus one, having a concrete model—the dots on the dice—to aid in counting helps make some of the activities more appropriate.

Many of the activities do not require writing numerals but can be modified to do so. For example, in the Double the Die Graph activity (page 16), children can write the equation in the box instead of placing a token. The Two-Dice Graph activity (page 30) can be used as a probability lesson. When children write all the possible addition equations that tossing two dice produces, they see which sums have the most possible outcomes and discover that a bell curve is produced.

Dice activities are an ideal way to differentiate classroom instruction. They can be introduced as whole-class instruction, used in small groups, individualized, used as an informal assessment, or provide a school–home link when shared with parents.

Questions to ask when using Dice Activities with an individual child, a small group, or a whole class. These questions will help you determine the child's level of understanding.

Dice Graph Activities (throughout book)

1. What is your favorite number?
2. What is the largest number you can toss with a die?
3. What is the smallest number you can toss with a die?
4. Say the column numbers from least to most.
5. Say the column numbers from most to least.
6. In the One-Die Graph activity (page 6), what number do you predict will be tossed?
7. What number do you think will get tossed the most?
8. What number do you think will get tossed the least?
9. Which column has the most? How do you know? How many does it have?
10. Which column has the least? How do you know? How many does it have?
11. Do any columns have the same amount? How do you know?
12. How many more does column ________ have than column ________?
13. Which has more, columns 2 and 3 or columns 1 and 6? How do you know?
14. If column __________ had 2 more, would it have the most?
15. What are the odd-number columns?
16. What are the even-number columns?
17. Do the odd-number columns have more than the even-number columns? How do you know?
18. How many more would you need to add so that the odd and even numbers have the same amount?
19. How many would you need to take away so that the odd and even numbers have the same amount?
20. Which columns have more than 2 but less than 6?
21. What is the largest number you can toss using two dice?
22. In the Two-Dice Graph activity (page 30), why is there no number 1?
23. What is the largest number you can toss using three dice?
24. What is the smallest number you can toss using three dice?
25. In the Three-Dice Graph activity (page 46), why are there no numbers 1 and 2?
26. In the One-Half-Die Graph activity (page 51), what numbers result in a whole number when cut in half?
27. What numbers result in a fraction or a whole number and a fraction when cut in half?

Notes to Teachers

Race to 25 (page 8) and Race to 50 (page 37)

1. How many spaces do you need to move to get to 25/50? How do you know?
2. Who is closer to 25/50? By how many spaces? How do you know?
3. Partway through the activity, ask: Who do you think will win? How do you know?

Race Back to 1 (page 9)

1. How many spaces do you need to move to get to 1? How do you know?
2. Who is closer to 1? By how many spaces? How do you know?

Place Value Addition (page 66), Place Value Subtraction (page 67), A Handful of Dice (page 70)

1. Which column seems the easiest to total? Why?
2. Which column seems the hardest? Why?
3. What are different ways to find the total of the ones column?
4. Why is this total of the Tens and Ones columns the same as the total of all the sums?

Two-Dice Switch (page 68)

1. Why are the numbers over 66 never crossed out?
2. What numbers less than 10 will not be crossed out? Why?
3. What happens when both dice have the same number of dots?
4. What numbers are most frequently tossed? Why?
5. What numbers are less likely to be tossed? Why?

Tic-Tac-Toe Activities (pages 73–93)

1. Is this an activity of luck or skill? Why?
2. What number was tossed the most? The least?
3. What are the most possible Tic-Tac-Toes (3 tokens in a row) you can get on one of the grids?
4. Which strategy works best? Trying to get the most 3 tokens in a row or trying to block your opponent from getting 3 in a row?

Meeting the NCTM Standards

NCTM STANDARDS	One-Die Activities Pages 3–25	Two-Dice Activities Pages 29–41	Three-Dice Activities Pages 45–48	Half-Die Activities Pages 51–56	Tens and Ones Activities Pages 59–70	Tic-Tac-Toe Activities Pages 73–93
Number and Operations						
Place value					✗	
Equivalent representations	✗		✗			
Fractions				✗	✗	✗
Addition and subtraction	✗	✗	✗	✗	✗	✗
Multiplication and division	✗					✗
Relationships between operations	✗	✗	✗	✗	✗	✗
Properties of operations	✗	✗	✗	✗	✗	✗
Fluency with operations	✗	✗	✗	✗	✗	✗
Using mental math	✗	✗	✗	✗	✗	✗
Estimation						
Selecting appropriate methods						
Data Analysis and Probability						
Predicting outcomes		✗	✗			✗
Problem Solving	✗	✗	✗	✗	✗	✗
Reasoning and Proof	✗	✗	✗	✗	✗	✗
Communication	✗	✗	✗	✗	✗	✗

One-Die Activities

Contents

Directions for One-Die Graph and Chart Activities

Objectives:

- Recognition of die dot patterns
- Recognition of numerals 1, 2, 3, 4, 5, 6
- Sequencing of numerals 1, 2, 3, 4, 5, 6
- Recording of numerals 1, 2, 3, 4, 5, 6

Materials

- 1 die
- Numeral cards 1 through 6
- Graph and chart activities using one die
- Tokens (tiles, cubes, chips)
- Pencils, markers, crayons

Warm-Up Activities

- Student tosses die and responds verbally with the numeral name.
- Student tosses die and responds by showing numeral card corresponding to the number pattern on the die.

die tossed card shown

NOTE how student arrives at answer:

- Does the student count each dot?
- Does the student recognize the number of dots?

Recording on Graphs

- Student tosses die and writes corresponding numeral on the graph.
- If students have not been instructed on correct numeral formation, they can color in the boxes on the graph or place a token on a box to indicate that dot pattern has been tossed.

  Activity is completed when one column of numerals is full.

Discussion

- What die pattern was tossed the most? The least?
- Is there a tie?
- Which number:

  has almost as many as ________?

  has the second most?

  has the second least?

  more than? less than? one more than? etc.
- Encourage the students to ask one another questions about the graphs.
- Make a large class graph and record daily class results of which die patterns occur the most (probability).

Chart Activities

- Each player chooses a color token.
- Players toss die.
- Highest number goes first.
- Player tosses die and performs operation (add one, subtract one, and so on).
- Player finds number on chart and places a token on number.
- If number has a token on it, player loses a turn.
- Count the tokens to see who wins.

Hundred Chart

1	2	3	4	5	6	7	8	9	10
11	12	13	14	15	16	17	18	19	20
21	22	23	24	25	26	27	28	29	30
31	32	33	34	35	36	37	38	39	40
41	42	43	44	45	46	47	48	49	50
51	52	53	54	55	56	57	58	59	60
61	62	63	64	65	66	67	68	69	70
71	72	73	74	75	76	77	78	79	80
81	82	83	84	85	86	87	88	89	90
91	92	93	94	95	96	97	98	99	100

One-Die Match Graph

How to Play

- Toss die.
- Mark a box in the column above the matching die image.

- *Variations depend on skill level and might include: coloring the box with crayon, making an "X" in the box, placing a chip or sticker in the box, writing the numeral in the box, and so on.*

Match the Die Pattern

- Each player chooses a color token (tiles, cubes, chips).

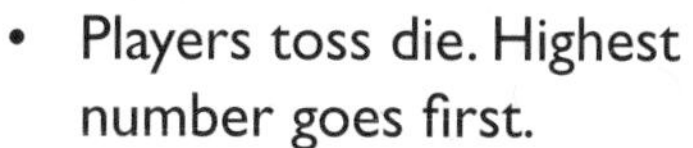

- Players toss die. Highest number goes first.

How to Play

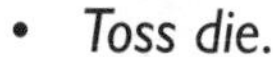

- *Toss die.*
- *Find the dot pattern on the chart.*

- *Place one token on the pattern.*
- *If pattern has a token on it, lose a turn.*
- *Count tokens to see who wins.*

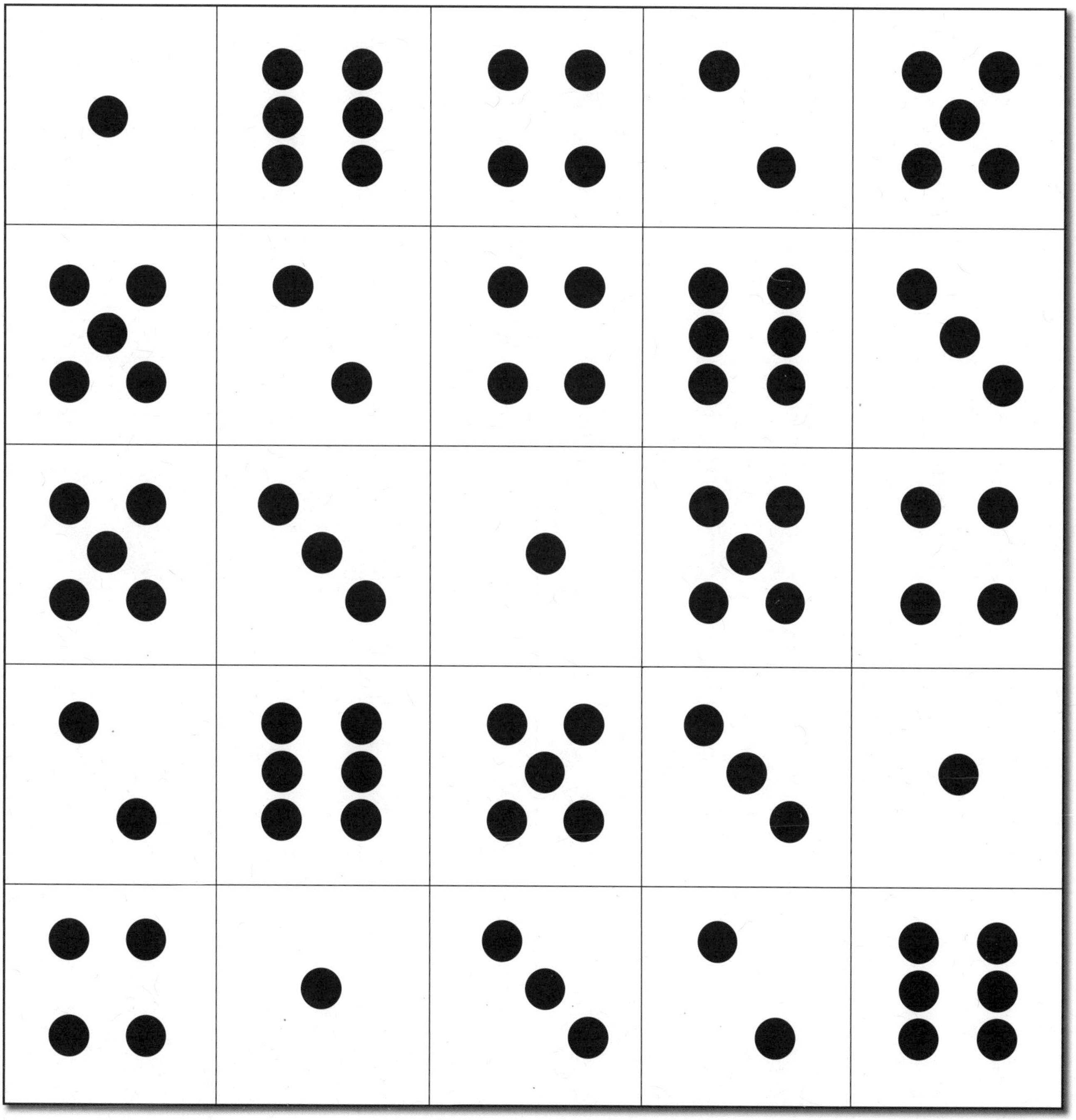

How to Play

One-Die Graph

- Toss a die.
- Mark a box in the column above the number tossed.

- *Variations depend on skill level and might include: coloring the box with crayon, making an "**X**" in the box, placing a chip or sticker in the box, writing the numeral in the box, and so on.*

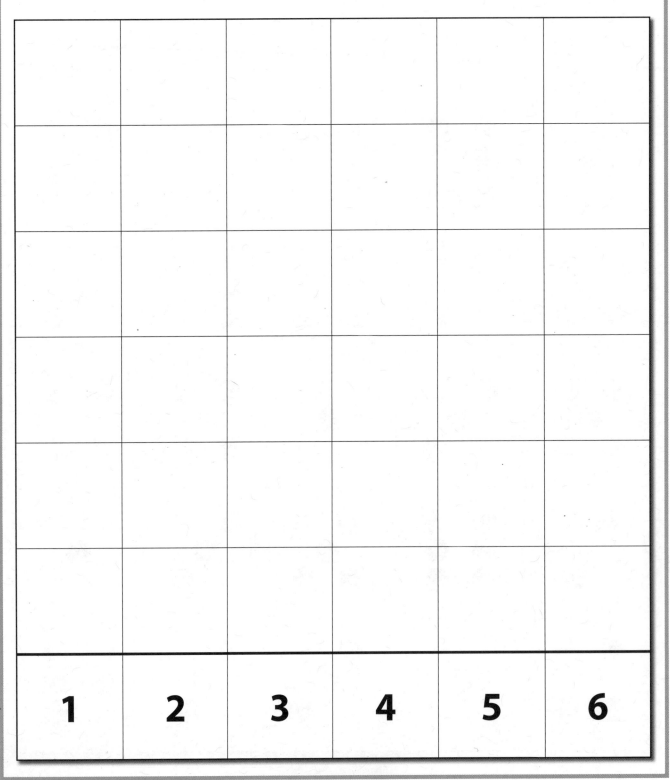

1	**2**	**3**	**4**	**5**	**6**

One-Die Chart

- Each player chooses a color token (tiles, cubes, chips).
- Players toss die. Highest number goes first.

- *Toss die.*
- *Find the number on the chart.*
- *Place one token on the pattern.*
- *If number has a token on it, lose a turn.*
- *Count tokens to see who wins.*

4	6	5	3	2
1	4	3	5	1
3	1	5	6	2
6	4	6	1	4
5	3	2	3	5
2	6	1	4	6

Race to 25

How to Play

- *Toss die. Highest goes first.*
- *Players take turns tossing die and moving their token that many boxes on the chart.*
- *Player must land exactly on **25** to win. First player to reach **25** wins.*

1	2	3	4	5
16	17	18	19	6
15	24	25	20	7
14	23	22	21	8
13	12	11	10	9

Race Back to 1

How to Play

- *Toss die. Highest goes first.*
- *Play begins on **25**.*
- *Players take turns tossing die and moving their token **backwards** that many boxes on the chart.*
- *Player must land exactly on **1** to win.*

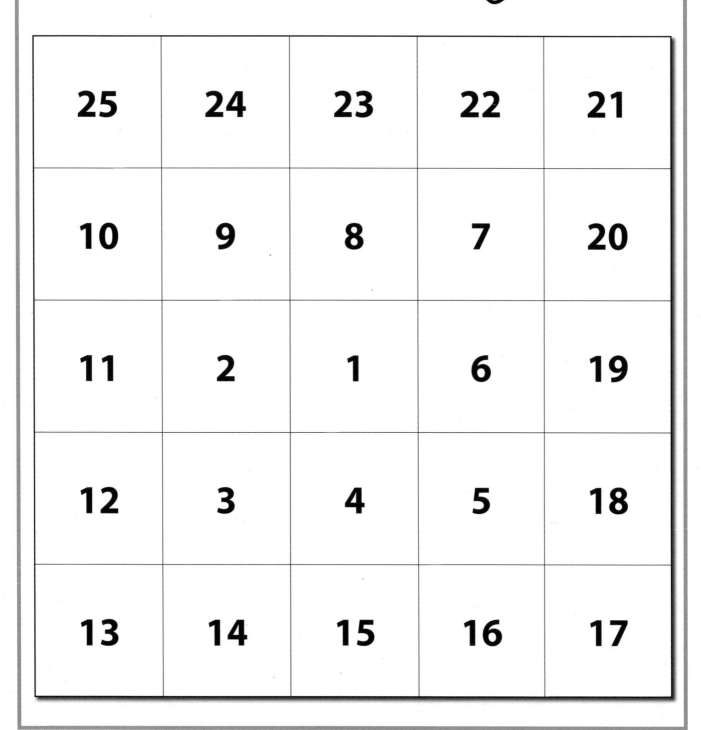

25	**24**	**23**	**22**	**21**
10	**9**	**8**	**7**	**20**
11	**2**	**1**	**6**	**19**
12	**3**	**4**	**5**	**18**
13	**14**	**15**	**16**	**17**

Die Plus One Graph

How to Play

- *Toss die.*
- *Add one.*
- *Fill in the box.*

2	**3**	**4**	**5**	**6**	**7**

Die Plus One Chart

- Each player chooses a color token (tiles, cubes, chips).
- Players toss die. Highest number goes first.

How to Play

- *Toss die.*
- *Add one.*
- *Find the number on the chart.*
- *Place one token on the number.*
- *If number has a token on it, lose a turn.*
- *Count tokens to see who wins.*

4	6	5	3	2
7	4	3	5	7
3	7	5	6	2
6	4	6	7	4
5	3	2	3	5
2	6	7	4	6

Die Plus Two Graph

How to Play

- *Toss die.*
- *Add two.*
- *Fill in the box.*

3	**4**	**5**	**6**	**7**	**8**

Die Plus Two Chart

- Each player chooses a color token (tiles, cubes, chips).
- Players toss die. Highest number goes first.

How to Play

- *Toss die.*
- *Add two.*
- *Find the number on the chart.*
- *Place one token on the number.*
- *If number has a token on it, lose a turn.*
- *Count tokens to see who wins.*

4	6	5	3	8
7	4	3	5	7
3	7	5	6	8
6	4	6	7	4
5	3	8	3	5
8	6	7	4	6

Die Minus One Graph

How to Play

- *Toss die.*
- *Subtract one.*
- *Fill in the box.*

0	**1**	**2**	**3**	**4**	**5**

Die Minus One Chart

- Each player chooses a color token (tiles, cubes, chips).
- Players toss die. Highest number goes first.

How to Play

- *Toss die.*
- *Subtract one.*
- *Find the number on the chart.*
- *Place one token on the number.*
- *If number has a token on it, lose a turn.*
- *Count tokens to see who wins.*

1	3	0	2	5
4	1	2	0	4
2	4	0	3	5
3	1	3	4	1
0	2	5	2	0
5	3	4	1	3

Double the Die Graph

How to Play

- *Toss die.* • *Double the amount.* • *Fill in the box.*

2	**4**	**6**	**8**	**10**	**12**

- Each player chooses a color token (tiles, cubes, chips).
- Players toss die. Highest number goes first.

Double the Die Chart

How to Play

- *Toss die.*
- *Double the amount.*
- *Find the number on the chart.*
- *Place one token on the number.*
- *If number has a token on it, lose a turn.*
- *Count tokens to see who wins.*

4	6	10	12	8
2	4	12	10	2
12	2	10	6	8
6	4	6	4	2
10	12	8	12	10
8	6	2	4	6

How to Play

1. Toss die.
2. Double the amount.
3. Add one.
4. Fill in the box.

Double the Die Plus One Graph

3	**5**	**7**	**9**	**11**	**13**

Double the Die Plus One Chart

- Each player chooses a color token (tiles, cubes, chips).
- Players toss die. Highest number goes first.

How to Play

- *Toss die.*
- *Double the amount.*
- *Add one.*
- *Find the number on the chart.*
- *Place one token on the number.*
- *If number has a token on it, lose a turn.*
- *Count tokens to see who wins.*

13	3	7	9	5
11	13	9	7	11
9	11	7	3	5
3	13	3	11	13
7	9	5	9	7
5	3	11	13	3

How to Play

1. Toss die.
2. Double the amount.
3. Subtract one.
4. Fill in the box.

Double the Die Minus One Graph

1	**3**	**5**	**7**	**9**	**11**

Double the Die Minus One Chart

- Each player chooses a color token (tiles, cubes, chips).
- Players toss die. Highest number goes first.

How to Play

- *Toss die.*
- *Double the amount.*
- *Subtract one.*
- *Find the number on the chart.*
- *Place one token on the number.*
- *If number has a token on it, lose a turn.*
- *Count tokens to see who wins.*

1	3	7	9	5
11	1	9	7	11
9	11	7	3	5
3	1	3	11	1
7	9	5	9	7
5	3	11	1	3

Die Plus One and Double Graph

How to Play

1. *Toss die.*
2. *Add one.*
3. *Double the amount.*
4. *Fill in the box.*

4	**6**	**8**	**10**	**12**	**14**

Die Plus One and Double Chart

- Each player chooses a color token (tiles, cubes, chips).
- Players toss die. Highest number goes first.

How to Play

- *Toss die.*
- *Add one.*
- *Double the amount.*
- *Find the number on the chart.*
- *Place one token on the number.*
- *If number has a token on it, lose a turn.*
- *Count tokens to see who wins.*

4	6	10	12	8
14	4	12	10	14
12	14	10	6	8
6	4	6	14	4
10	12	8	12	10
8	6	14	4	6

Odd / Even Die Graph

How to Play

- *Toss die.*
- ***Odd number toss:***
  Write the odd number in the odd-number column or place a token in the odd-number column.
- ***Even number toss:***
  Write the even number in the even-number column or place a token in the even-number column.

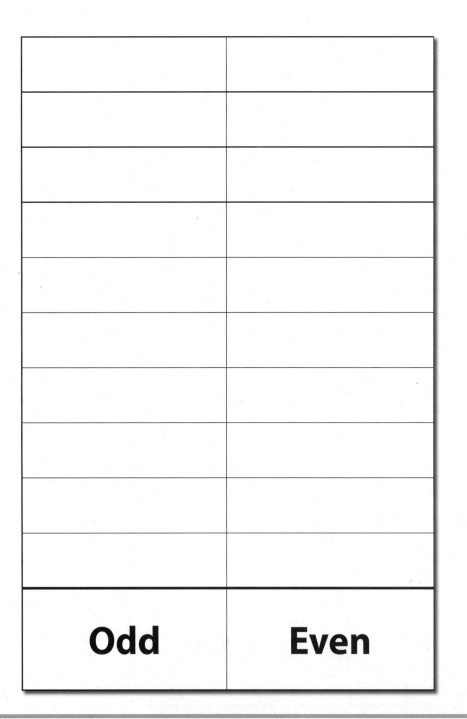

Odd	**Even**

Odd / Even Die Chart

- Each player chooses a color token (tiles, cubes, chips).
- Players toss die.
- Highest number goes first.

How to Play

- *Toss die.*
- *If number tossed is odd, place token on a box that says* ***odd.***
- *If number tossed is even, place token on a box that says* ***even.***
- *When all spaces are covered, count tokens to see who wins.*

even	**odd**	**even**	**odd**	**even**
odd	**even**	**odd**	**even**	**odd**
even	**odd**	**even**	**odd**	**even**
odd	**even**	**odd**	**even**	**odd**
even	**odd**	**even**	**odd**	**even**
odd	**even**	**odd**	**even**	**odd**

Two-Dice Activities

Contents:

Directions for Two-Dice Graph and Chart Activities

Objectives:

- Recognition of numerals 1 through 12
- Recognition of number patterns 1 through 12
- Recording of numerals 2 through 12
- Recognition of odd and even numbers

Materials

- 2 dice
- Red and white dice
- Numeral cards 1 through 18
- Graph and chart activities using two dice
- Tokens (tiles, cubes, chips)
- Pencils, markers, crayons

Warm-Up Activities

- Student tosses two dice, finds the sum of the dots on the dice, and responds verbally with the numeral name.
- Student tosses two dice and responds by showing the numeral card with the sum of the two dice.

NOTE how student arrives at the sum:

- Does the student count each dot?
- Does the student recognize the pattern on a die and continue counting from there?
- Does the student recognize the pattern combination with no indication of counting the dots? This is an indication that the student is conserving number.

Recording on Graphs

- Student tosses two dice and writes corresponding numeral for the sum of the dice above the corresponding numeral on the graph.
- If students have not been instructed on correct numeral formation, they can color in the boxes on the graph or place a token on a box to indicate that sum has been tossed.
- Activity is completed when one column of numerals is full.

NOTE

- Why is there no 1 on the two-dice graph?

Discussion

- What die pattern was tossed the most? The least?
- Is there a tie?
- Which number:

  has almost as many as ________?

  has the second most?

  has the second least?

  more than? less than? one more than? etc.
- Encourage the students to ask one another questions about the graphs.
- Make a large class graph and record daily class results of which die patterns occur the most (probability).

Chart Activities

- Each player chooses a color token.
- Players toss dice.
- Highest number goes first.
- Player tosses dice and performs operation (adds, subtracts, halves, and so on).
- Player finds the number on the chart and places a token on number.
- If number has a token on it, player loses a turn.
- Count the tokens to see who wins.

Hundred Chart

1	2	3	4	5	6	7	8	9	10
11	12	13	14	15	16	17	18	19	20
21	22	23	24	25	26	27	28	29	30
31	32	33	34	35	36	37	38	39	40
41	42	43	44	45	46	47	48	49	50
51	52	53	54	55	56	57	58	59	60
61	62	63	64	65	66	67	68	69	70
71	72	73	74	75	76	77	78	79	80
81	82	83	84	85	86	87	88	89	90
91	92	93	94	95	96	97	98	99	100

Two-Dice Graph

How to Play

- Toss two dice and find the sum.
- Place an *X* in the column above the sum.

- *A variation is to write the equation in the box—for example, if 2 and 3 are tossed, find the column over the 5 and write "2 + 3."*

2	**3**	**4**	**5**	**6**	**7**	**8**	**9**	**10**	**11**	**12**

Two-Dice Chart

- Each player chooses a color token (tiles, cubes, chips).
- Each player tosses 2 dice and adds dots. Highest number goes first.

How to Play

- *Toss 2 dice. Find the sum.*
- *Find the number on the chart.*
- *Place one token on the number.*
- *If number has a token on it, lose a turn.*
- *Count tokens to see who wins.*

9	11	12	2	7	3
6	4	9	5	10	6
5	6	10	8	2	9
11	3	8	7	8	12
7	6	12	2	3	4
10	11	5	8	4	7

Subtraction Graph

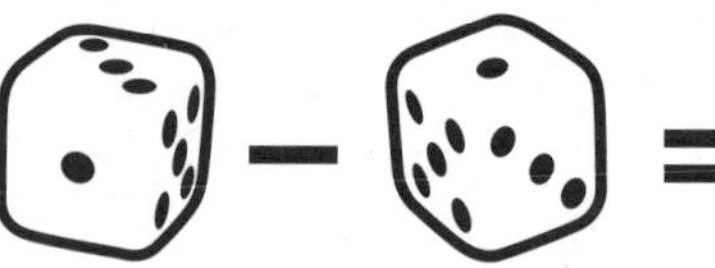

How to Play

- *Toss 2 dice and write the difference between the pair of dice on the graph in the corresponding column.*
- *Activity is completed when one column is full.*

0	**1**	**2**	**3**	**4**	**5**

Sum / Difference Activity

Toss 2 dice and write the 2 numbers. It is important to write the ***higher number first!***	**SUM** plus (+)	**DIFFERENCE** minus (–)
Example: If you roll 2 and 3.... **3, 2**	**3 + 2 = 5**	**3 – 2 = 1**

Sum / Difference Activity

*Toss 2 dice and write the 2 numbers. It is important to write the **higher number first!***	SUM plus (+)	DIFFERENCE minus (–)

Two-Dice Addition Grid

How to Play

- *Each player has a chart.*
- *Players take turns tossing red and white dice.*
- *Player finds the SUM of the dice.*
- *Records the sum in the grid.*
- *If box is filled, loses a turn.*
- *First to complete the chart wins.*

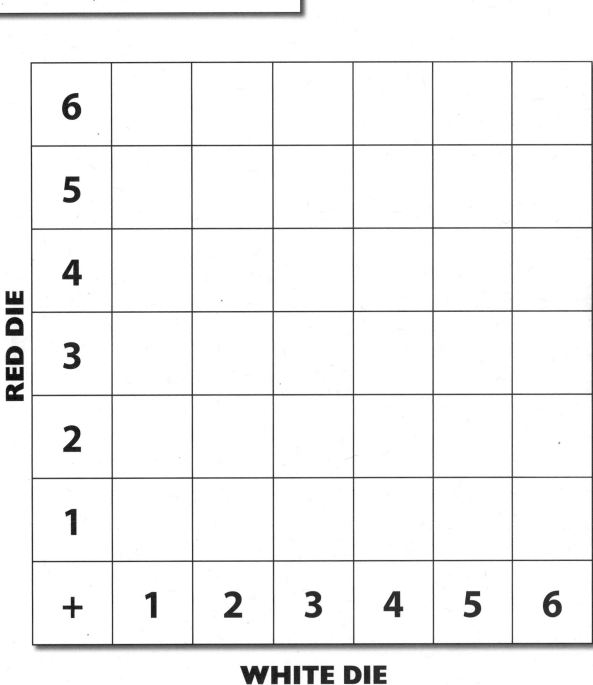

+ =

RED DIE

6						
5						
4						
3						
2						
1						
+	1	2	3	4	5	6

WHITE DIE

Two-Dice Subtraction Grid

How to Play

- *Each player has a chart.*
- *Players take turns tossing red and white dice.*
- *Player finds the DIFFERENCE (subtracts smaller amount from larger amount).*
- *Records the difference on the grid.*
- *If box is filled, loses a turn.*
- *First to complete the chart wins.*

RED DIE

6						
5						
4						
3						
2						
1						
–	**1**	**2**	**3**	**4**	**5**	**6**

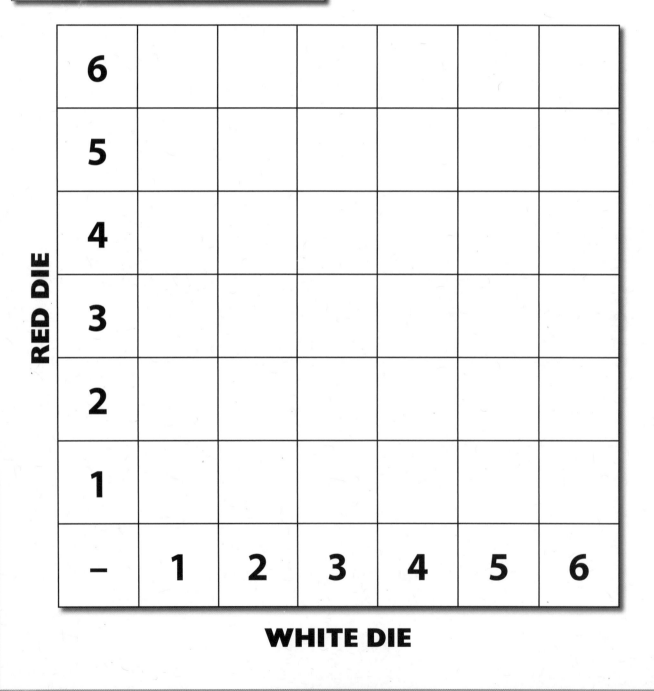

WHITE DIE

Race to 50

How to Play

- Toss die. Highest goes first.
- Player places token at 1, tosses die, moves that many spaces toward 50.
- Players take turns tossing die and moving their token that many boxes on the chart.
- Player must land exactly on 1 to win.

Variations

- *Toss die. Add 1 to it.*
- *Toss die. Add 2 to it.*
- *Toss die. Double it.*
- *Toss 2 dice.*

1	2	3	4	5	6	7	8	9	10
20	19	18	17	16	15	14	13	12	11
21	22	23	24	25	26	27	28	29	30
40	39	38	37	36	35	34	33	32	31
41	42	43	44	45	46	47	48	49	50

Race Back! 50 to 1

How to Play

- *Toss die. Highest goes first.*
- *Player places token at 50, tosses die, moves that many spaces toward 1.*
- *Player must land exactly on 1 to win.*

Variations

- *Toss die. Add 1 to it.*
- *Toss die. Add 2 to it.*
- *Toss die. Double it.*
- *Toss 2 dice.*

50	49	48	47	46	45	44	43	42	41
31	32	33	34	35	36	37	38	39	40
30	29	28	27	26	25	24	23	22	21
11	12	13	14	15	16	17	18	19	20
10	9	8	7	6	5	4	3	2	1

Two-Dice Odd / Even Die Chart

- Each player chooses a color token (tiles, cubes, chips).
- Players toss die.
- Highest number goes first.

How to Play

- *Toss dice. Find the sum.*
- *If number tossed is odd, place token on a box that says* **odd.**
- *If number tossed is even, place token on a box that says* **even.**
- *When all spaces are covered, count tokens to see who wins.*

even	odd	even	odd	even
odd	even	odd	even	odd
even	odd	even	odd	even
odd	even	odd	even	odd
even	odd	even	odd	even
odd	even	odd	even	odd

How to Play

- *Toss a pair of dice and find the sum.*
- *Is the sum ODD or EVEN?*
- *If the sum is an EVEN number, mark a box in the column above the EVEN number.*
- *If the sum is an ODD number, toss again.*

Two-Dice EVEN Number Graph

2	**4**	**6**	**8**	**10**	**12**

How to Play

- *Toss a pair of dice and find the sum.*
- *Is the sum ODD or EVEN?*
- *If the sum is an ODD number, mark a box in the column above the ODD number.*
- *If the sum is an EVEN number, toss again.*

Two-Dice ODD Number Graph

3	**5**	**7**	**9**	**11**

Three-Dice Activities

Contents:

Directions for Three-Dice Graph and Chart Activities

Objectives:

- Recognition of numerals 1 through 18
- Recognition of number patterns 1 through 18
- Recording of numerals 3 through 18
- Recognition of odd and even numbers

Materials

- 3 dice
- Numeral cards 1 through 18
- Graph and chart activities using three dice
- Tokens (tiles, cubes, chips)
- Pencils, markers, crayons

Warm-Up Activities

- Student tosses three dice, finds the sum of the dots on the dice, and responds verbally with the numeral name.
- Student tosses three dice and responds by showing the numeral card with the sum of the three dice.

NOTE how student arrives at the sum:

- Does the student count each dot?
- Does the student recognize the pattern on a die and continue counting from there?
- Does the student recognize the pattern combination with no indication of counting the dots? This is an indication that the student is conserving number.

Recording on Graphs

- Student tosses three dice and writes corresponding numeral for the sum of the dice above the corresponding numeral on the graph.
- If students have not been instructed on correct numeral formation, they can color in the boxes on the graph or place a token on a box to indicate that sum has been tossed.
- Activity is completed when one column of numerals is full.

NOTE

- Why is there no 1 or 2 on the three-dice graph?

Discussion

- What die pattern was tossed the most? The least?
- Is there a tie?
- Which number:

  has almost as many as ________?

  has the second most?

  has the second least?

  more than? less than? one more than? etc.
- Encourage the students to ask one another questions about the graphs.
- Make a large class graph and record daily class results of which die patterns occur the most (probability).

Chart Activities

- Each player chooses a color token.
- Players toss dice.
- Highest number goes first.
- Player tosses dice and performs operation (adds, subtracts, halves, and so on).
- Player finds the number on the chart and places a token on number.
- If number has a token on it, player loses a turn.
- Count the tokens to see who wins.

Hundred Chart

1	2	3	4	5	6	7	8	9	10
11	12	13	14	15	16	17	18	19	20
21	22	23	24	25	26	27	28	29	30
31	32	33	34	35	36	37	38	39	40
41	42	43	44	45	46	47	48	49	50
51	52	53	54	55	56	57	58	59	60
61	62	63	64	65	66	67	68	69	70
71	72	73	74	75	76	77	78	79	80
81	82	83	84	85	86	87	88	89	90
91	92	93	94	95	96	97	98	99	100

Three-Dice Graph

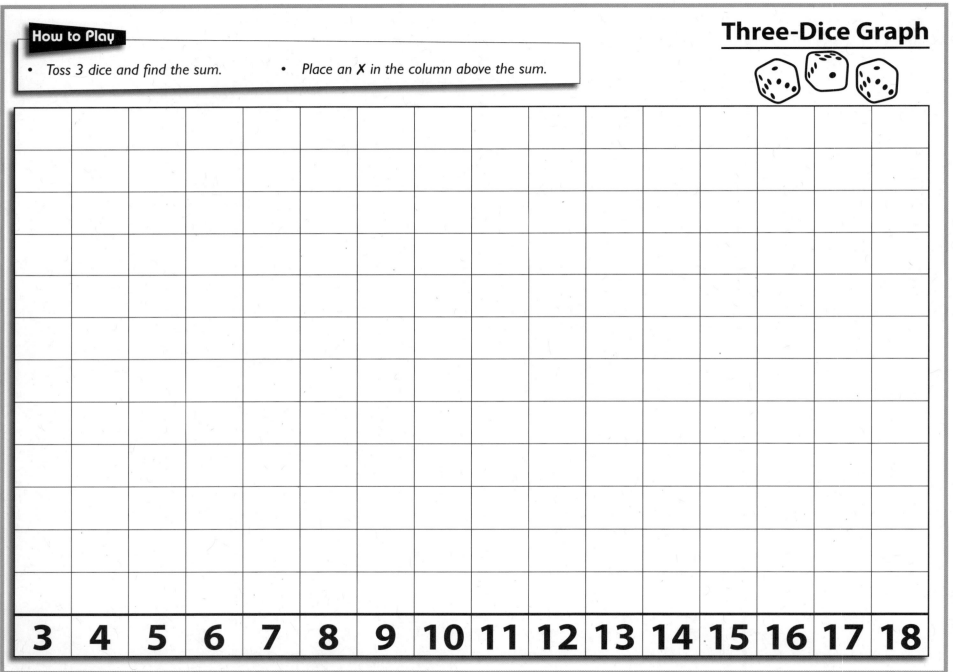

How to Play

- *Toss 3 dice and find the sum.*
- *Place an **X** in the column above the sum.*

3	**4**	**5**	**6**	**7**	**8**	**9**	**10**	**11**	**12**	**13**	**14**	**15**	**16**	**17**	**18**

Three-Dice Toss – Addition

How to Play

- *Toss 3 dice. Find the sum.*
- *Find the sum on the chart.*
- *Place your color token on that number.*
- *Lose a turn if you cannot place a token on the chart.*
- *Player with the most tokens wins.*

8	13	10	16	5
9	3	11	13	12
10	14	15	9	10
13	11	7	18	6
9	17	4	12	14

Three-Dice Toss – Addition

(to fill in)

How to Play

- *Fill in the chart with random numbers from 3 to18.*
- *Toss 3 dice. Find the sum.*
- *Find the total on the chart.*
- *Place your color token on that number.*
- *Lose a turn if you cannot place a token on the chart.*
- *Player with the most tokens wins.*

Half-Die Activities

Contents:

Directions for Half-Die Graph and Chart Activities

Objectives:

- Conceptualize half of a number
- Find half of numbers 1 through 18
- Recognize a mixed number as half of an odd number
- Recognize that half of an even number results in a whole number
- Recognize that half of an odd number results in the fraction $\frac{1}{2}$ or a whole number and the fraction $\frac{1}{2}$
- Practice adding numbers mentally and then dividing by 2
- Develop a sense of numbers as whole and mixed numbers

Materials

- 1 die, 2 dice, or 3 dice
- One-half-die graph and chart activities
- Tokens (tiles, cubes, chips)
- Pencils, color markers

Warm-Up Activity: One-Half-Die Graph

- Make an overhead of the One-Half-Die Graph or sketch it on the board.
- Teacher tosses die and asks, "How many dots are on the die?" (6)
- A student gathers that many tokens and finds half of the number of tokens and says, "Half of 6 is 3."
- Student finds the number 3 on the graph and writes a 3 in the box above the 3 on the graph.
- Teacher tosses the die again and asks, "How many dots are on the die?" (5)
- A student gathers that many tokens, finds half of the number of tokens, and says, "Half of 5 is 2 and a half."
- Student finds the number $2\frac{1}{2}$ on the graph and writes $2\frac{1}{2}$ in the box above the $2\frac{1}{2}$ on the graph.
- Activity is completed when one column of numerals is full.

Warm-Up Activity: Half Two-Dice Graph

- Teacher makes a large class graph of the One-Half of Two Dice Graph.
- Class is divided into two teams, and each team chooses a color marker.
- Teacher tosses 2 dice and asks, "How many dots are on the dice?" ($5+3=8$)
- A student from one team gathers that many tokens, finds half of the number of tokens, and says, "Half of 8 is 4."
- Student finds the number 4 on the class graph and, using the team color, writes a 4 in the box above the 4 on the class graph
- Teacher tosses 2 dice and asks, "How many dots are on the dice?" ($5+6=11$)
- A student from the other team gathers that many tokens, finds half of the number of tokens, and says, "Half of 11 is $5\frac{1}{2}$."
- Student finds the number $5\frac{1}{2}$ on the class graph and, using the team color, writes a $5\frac{1}{2}$ in the box above the $5\frac{1}{2}$ on the class graph.
- Activity is completed when one column of numerals is full.

Discussion

- What die pattern was tossed the most? The least?
- Is there a tie?
- Which number:

  has almost as many as __________?

  has the second most? has the second least?

  more than? less than? one more than? etc.
- What numbers result in a whole number when cut in half?
- What numbers result in a fraction or a whole number and fraction when cut in half?
- Have the class discuss ways to total each of the columns (count the whole numbers, then count the halves, and add the sum of the halves to the sum of the whole numbers).

How to Play

- *Toss die.*
- *Find half of the number.*
- *Fill in the box.*

One-Half-Die Graph

$\frac{1}{2}$	1	$1\frac{1}{2}$	2	$2\frac{1}{2}$	3

One-Half-Die Chart

- Each player chooses a color token (tiles, cubes, chips).
- Each player tosses a die. Highest number goes first.

How to Play

- *Toss die. Find half of the number.*
- *Find the number on the chart.*
- *Place one token on the number.*
- *If number has a token on it, lose a turn.*
- *Count tokens to see who wins.*

$\frac{1}{2}$	$1\frac{1}{2}$	2	$2\frac{1}{2}$	$1\frac{1}{2}$
3	$\frac{1}{2}$	$2\frac{1}{2}$	2	3
$2\frac{1}{2}$	3	2	1	$1\frac{1}{2}$
1	$\frac{1}{2}$	1	3	$\frac{1}{2}$
2	$2\frac{1}{2}$	$1\frac{1}{2}$	$2\frac{1}{2}$	2
$1\frac{1}{2}$	1	3	$\frac{1}{2}$	1

One-Half of Two-Dice Graph

How to Play

- Toss two dice and find the sum.
- Half of the sum is how many dots? Fill in the box.

$\frac{1}{2}$	1	$1\frac{1}{2}$	2	$2\frac{1}{2}$	3	$3\frac{1}{2}$	4	$4\frac{1}{2}$	5	$5\frac{1}{2}$	6

One-Half of Two-Dice Chart

- Each player chooses a color token (tiles, cubes, chips).
- Players toss 2 dice and find the sum. Highest number goes first.

How to Play

- *Toss 2 dice. Find the sum; then find half of the sum.*
- *Find the number on the chart.*
- *Place a token on the number.*
- *If number has a token on it, lose a turn.*
- *Count tokens to see who wins.*

$3\frac{1}{2}$	1	$1\frac{1}{2}$	2	$2\frac{1}{2}$	3
$3\frac{1}{2}$	4	$4\frac{1}{2}$	5	$5\frac{1}{2}$	6
5	6	$5\frac{1}{2}$	$3\frac{1}{2}$	2	$4\frac{1}{2}$
1	3	4	$2\frac{1}{2}$	$3\frac{1}{2}$	$1\frac{1}{2}$
$2\frac{1}{2}$	6	$1\frac{1}{2}$	2	3	4
$5\frac{1}{2}$	1	5	$3\frac{1}{2}$	$\frac{1}{2}$	3

One-Half of Three-Dice Graph

How to Play

- Toss two dice and find the sum.
- Half of the sum is how many dots? Fill in the box.

$\frac{1}{2}$	1	$1\frac{1}{2}$	2	$2\frac{1}{2}$	3	$3\frac{1}{2}$	4	$4\frac{1}{2}$	5	$5\frac{1}{2}$	6	$6\frac{1}{2}$	7	$7\frac{1}{2}$	8	$8\frac{1}{2}$	9

- Each player chooses a color token (tiles, cubes, chips).
- Players toss 3 dice and find the sum. Highest number goes first.

One-Half of Three-Dice Chart

How to Play

- *Toss 3 dice. Find the sum; then find half of the sum.*
- *Find the number on the chart.*
- *Place a token on the number.*
- *If number has a token on it, lose a turn.*
- *Count tokens to see who wins.*

$8\frac{1}{2}$	4	$1\frac{1}{2}$	$5\frac{1}{2}$	5	9	3
$7\frac{1}{2}$	$3\frac{1}{2}$	2	8	$2\frac{1}{2}$	$4\frac{1}{2}$	6
9	$5\frac{1}{2}$	7	5	$7\frac{1}{2}$	$6\frac{1}{2}$	8
$2\frac{1}{2}$	3	$8\frac{1}{2}$	6	7	$4\frac{1}{2}$	2
4	$6\frac{1}{2}$	2	$5\frac{1}{2}$	$1\frac{1}{2}$	7	$6\frac{1}{2}$
8	$4\frac{1}{2}$	6	9	$3\frac{1}{2}$	$2\frac{1}{2}$	3
$1\frac{1}{2}$	5	$3\frac{1}{2}$	$7\frac{1}{2}$	$5\frac{1}{2}$	4	$8\frac{1}{2}$

Tens and Ones Activities

Contents:

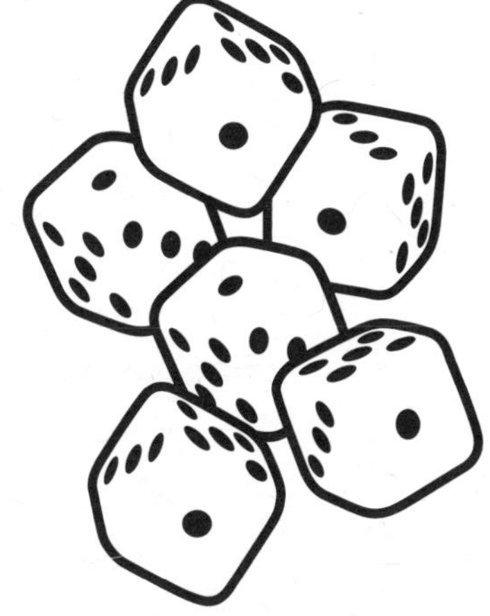

Directions for Tens and Ones Activities

Objectives:

- Conceptualize sets of 10
- Add 10 to numbers 1 through 18
- Recognize number patterns when adding 10 to a number (unit numeral remains the same)
- Recognize number patterns when subtracting a number from a number ending in zero—for example, 20 – 3 = 17
- Develop a sense of number and number patterns 1 through 100

Materials

- 10–15 dice
- Red and white dice
- Tens/ones card
- Hundred Chart
- Graph and chart activities
- Tokens (tiles, cubes, chips)
- Pencils, markers, crayons

Warm-Up Activity: Dot on Die = 10

- Student tosses die, says how many dots.
- With each dot representing 10, student counts by tens to find out how many tens are represented by the die toss.

Warm-Up Activity: Grouping by 10

- Student tosses 10–15 dice.
- Student organizes dice in groups whose sum is 10—for example, 6, 4; 5, 5; 2, 3, 5; 2, 2, 6.
- Student counts the groups of 10 and adds the dice left over to find the value of the toss.

Discussion: Graph and Chart Activities

- What die pattern was tossed the most? The least?
- Is there a tie?
- Which number:
  has almost as many as ________?
  has the second most? has the second least?
  more than? less than? one more than? etc.
- Make a large class graph of the Die Plus Ten Chart and play the activity as a class. Discuss ways to find the total of each column.

Discussion: Place Value Addition and Subtraction, Handful of Dice

- Discuss ways to find the total of each of the three columns.
- Which column seems the easiest to total? Why?
- Which column seems the hardest? Why?
- What are different ways to find the total of the ones column?
- Add the Tens total to the Ones total. Why is this total the same as the total of all the sums?

Discussion: Two-Dice Switch

- What die pattern was tossed the most? The least?
- What are the most numerals that can be crossed off in a toss?
- What tosses result in no numerals being crossed off?
- What is the least number of numerals, aside from zero, that can be crossed off in a toss?
- What number combinations result in only two numerals being crossed off?
- What is the highest number that can be crossed off?
- What is the lowest number that can be crossed off?
- Are there any other numbers between 1 and 66 (besides 1) that cannot be crossed off?
- Is this a fair game? Explain.

How to Play

- *Toss die.*
- *Add 10.*
- *Fill in the box.*

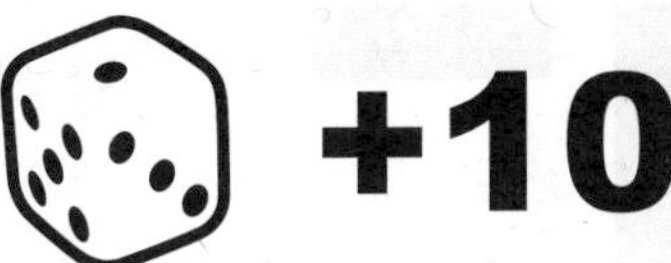

Die Plus Ten Graph

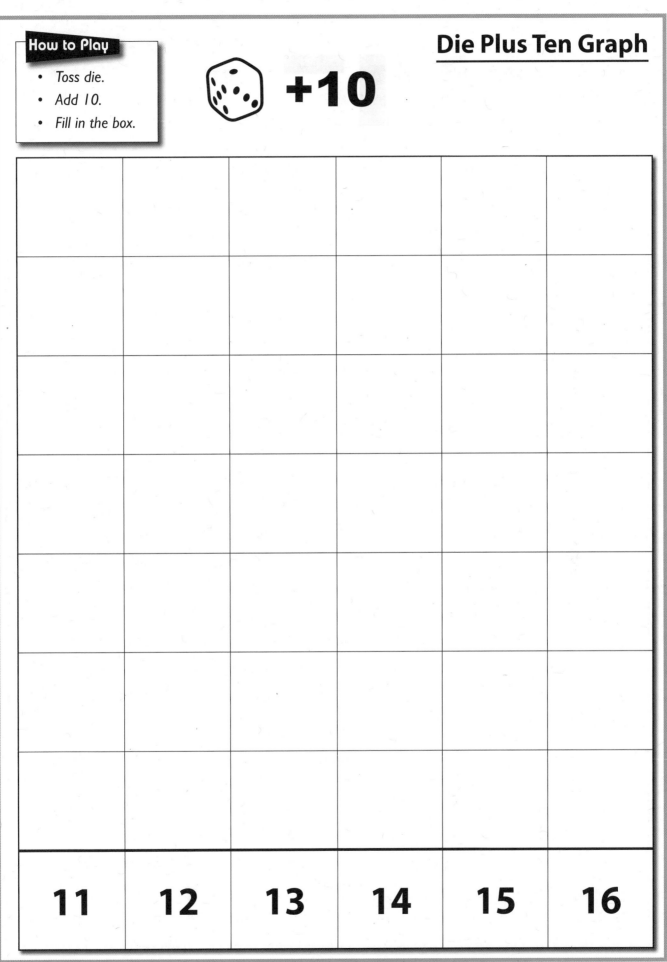

11	**12**	**13**	**14**	**15**	**16**

Die Plus Ten Chart

- Each player chooses a color token (tiles, cubes, chips).
- Players toss die and add 10. Highest number goes first.

How to Play

- *Toss die and add 10 to the number.*
- *Find the sum on the chart and place a token on that number.*
- *If number has token on it, lose turn.*
- *Count tokens to see who wins.*

11	12	13	14	15
16	11	15	13	16
15	16	11	12	13
12	11	12	16	11
14	15	13	15	14
13	14	16	15	12

Two Dice Plus Ten Graph

How to Play

- Toss 2 dice and find the sum.
- Add 10 to the sum.
- Fill in the box.

12	**13**	**14**	**15**	**16**	**17**	**18**	**19**	**20**	**21**	**22**

Two Dice Plus Ten Chart

- Each player chooses a color token (tiles, cubes, chips).
- Players toss dice, find the sum, and add 10.
- Highest number goes first.

How to Play

- Toss two dice, find the sum, and add 10.
- Find the sum on the chart, and place a token on that number.
- If number has token on it, lose a turn.
- Count tokens to see who wins.

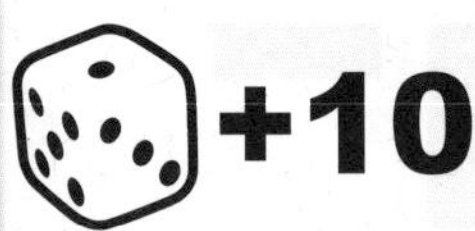

12	13	14	15	16	17
18	19	20	21	22	21
20	19	18	17	16	14
13	12	17	18	16	14
19	13	20	17	18	16

Three Dice Plus Ten Graph

How to Play

- Toss 3 dice and find the sum.
- Add 10 to the sum.
- Fill in the box.

13	14	15	16	17	18	19	20	21	22	23	24	25	26	27	28

Three Dice Plus Ten Chart

- Each player chooses a color token (tiles, cubes, chips).
- Players toss 3 dice, find the sum, and add 10. Highest sum goes first.

How to Play

- *Toss 3 dice, find the sum, and add 10.*
- *Find the sum on the chart.*
- *Place a token on the sum.*
- *If sum has a token on it, lose a turn.*
- *Count tokens to see who wins.*

13	21	26	22	19	23
25	15	17	20	18	14
18	20	19	23	21	18
16	24	22	15	25	28
20	26	21	19	23	24
27	21	16	22	17	20

Place Value Dice Addition Activity Page 66

1. Student tosses red and white dice and places the red die on the **Tens** box and the white die on the **Ones** box.

Tens	Ones
⚃	⚁

2. Student says how many tens and records it in the **Tens** column.

4

3. Student says how many ones and records it in the **Ones** column.

2

4. Student records the number sentence **40 + 2** in the **Number Sentence** column and records the sum, **42**, in the **Sum** column.

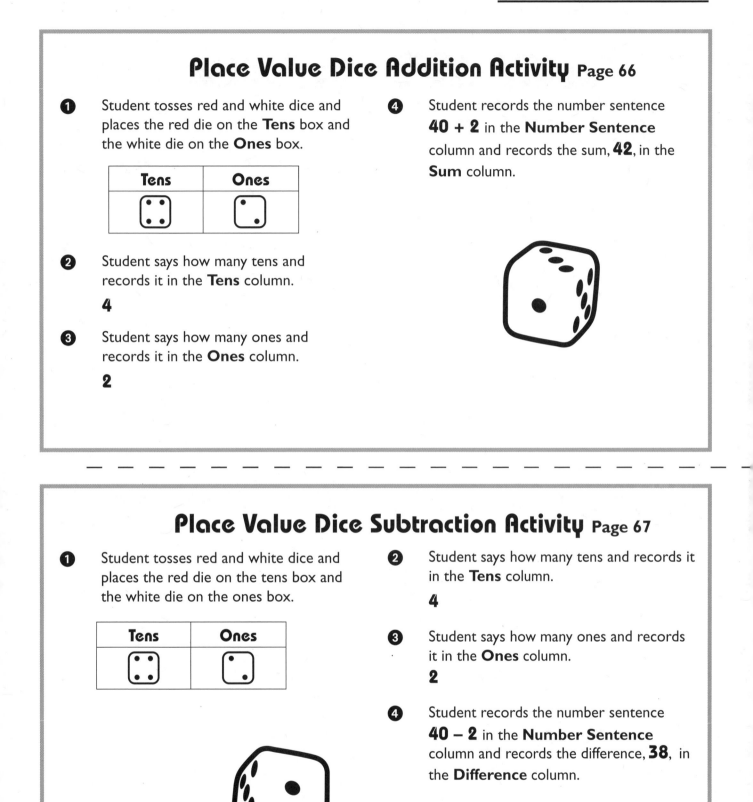

Place Value Dice Subtraction Activity Page 67

1. Student tosses red and white dice and places the red die on the tens box and the white die on the ones box.

Tens	Ones
⚃	⚁

2. Student says how many tens and records it in the **Tens** column.

4

3. Student says how many ones and records it in the **Ones** column.

2

4. Student records the number sentence **40 – 2** in the **Number Sentence** column and records the difference, **38**, in the **Difference** column.

Place Value Dice Addition Activity

Red Die	White Die	Number Sentence	+
Tens	Ones		Sum
Example: 4	2	40 + 2	42

Place Value Dice Subtraction Activity

Red Die	White Die	Number Sentence	–
Tens	Ones		Difference
Example: 4	2	40 – 2	38

Two-Dice Switch

Object

To cross off the most numbers on a Hundred Chart

Materials

- *Hundred Chart*
- *Make Tens/Ones cards (see sample in direction #3)*
- *Two different-color markers or crayons*
- *Two dice*

Directions:

1. Players select color crayon.
2. Each player tosses dice. Highest sum goes first.
3. Player 1 tosses dice. Places a die on **Tens** side on card. Places other die on **Ones** side.

Tens	Ones

4. Player 1 – adds 40 + 2 = 42, crosses off 42 on Hundred Chart in crayon.
5. Player 1 – subtracts 40 – 2 = 38, crosses off 38 on Hundred Chart.
6. Player 1 – switches dice on card. Places 2 die on **Tens** side of chart and 4 die on **Ones** side of chart.
7. Player 1 – adds 20 + 4 = 24, crosses off 24 on Hundred Chart.
8. Player 1 – subtracts 20 – 4 = 16, crosses off 16 on Hundred Chart.
9. Player 2 tosses dice, repeats steps of player 1.
10. When no more numerals can be crossed off, players count numerals each crossed off to determine the winner.

1	2	3	4	5	6	7	8	9	10
11	12	13	14	15	16	17	18	19	20
21	22	23	24	25	26	27	28	29	30
31	32	33	34	35	36	37	38	39	40
41	42	43	44	45	46	47	48	49	50
51	52	53	54	55	56	57	58	59	60
61	62	63	64	65	66	67	68	69	70
71	72	73	74	75	76	77	78	79	80
81	82	83	84	85	86	87	88	89	90
91	92	93	94	95	96	97	98	99	100

Hundred Chart

1	2	3	4	5	6	7	8	9	10
11	12	13	14	15	16	17	18	19	20
21	22	23	24	25	26	27	28	29	30
31	32	33	34	35	36	37	38	39	40
41	42	43	44	45	46	47	48	49	50
51	52	53	54	55	56	57	58	59	60
61	62	63	64	65	66	67	68	69	70
71	72	73	74	75	76	77	78	79	80
81	82	83	84	85	86	87	88	89	90
91	92	93	94	95	96	97	98	99	100

A Handful of Dice

Object

- Practice combinations that equal 10.
- Practice adding tens and ones.
- For assessment.

Materials

- *A bucket of dice*
- *Pencil*
- *Recording sheet*

Directions:

1. Student takes a handful of dice from the bucket.
2. Student drops dice on table.
3. Student groups together dice that equal 10 (for example, 5 + 5, 6 + 4, 3 + 2 + 5).
4. Student counts the sets of tens and adds the dice left over to find the total of all the dice. (Example: 3 sets of 10 plus 8 left over = 38)

This activity may be used for practice/ assessment:

- How many sets of tens? What is left over?
- What is the total of all the dice?

It may also be used as a recording activity:

- How many sets of tens? How many ones are left over? What is your total?

Tens	Ones	Total

Tic-Tac-Toe Activities

Contents:

Directions for Tic-Tac-Toe Activities

Objectives:

- Review number concepts developed through the graph and chart activities
- Practice computation
- Develop number sense
- Develop game strategy
- Develop communication and cooperation skills

Materials

- Dice
- Tic-Tac-Toe grids
- Tens/ones card
- Tokens (tiles, cubes, chips)
- Pencils, markers

Warm-Up Activity: Tic-Tac-Toe

- Make an overhead of one of the activities or sketch it on the board. Play against the class, following the directions.
- Player chooses an X or O.
- Players toss die. Highest number goes first.
- Player tosses die or dice and computes answer.
- Player finds the new number on the grid and places an X or O on it.
- If the number has a token on it, player loses a turn.
- Player winning 2 out of 3 games wins.

Discussion

- Is this a game of luck or skill? Why?
- What numbers do you need to toss to win?
- Which number was tossed the most?
- Which number was tossed the least?

Warm-Up Activity: 4-Grid Tic-Tac-Toe

- Make an overhead of one of the 4-Grid Tic-Tac-Toe activities. Play the game against the class, following the directions.
- Player chooses an X or O.
- Players toss die. Highest number goes first.
- Player tosses die or dice and computes the answer.
- Player finds the new number on any of the grids and places a token on it.
- If the number is not available on any of the grids, player loses a turn.
- When no more winning plays are possible on any of the grids, players count their Tic-Tac-Toe scores (3 tokens in a row) to find the winner.

Discussion

- What are the most possible Tic-Tac-Toes you can get on one of the grids?
- Which strategy works best—trying to get the most 3 tokens in a row or trying to block your opponent from getting 3 in a row?

Die Plus One Tic-Tac-Toe

- Each player chooses a color token (tiles, cubes, chips).
- Players each toss die. Highest number goes first.

- *Toss die.*
- *Add one to the number of dots on the die.*
- *Player finds the new number on the grid and places a token on it.*
- *If number has a token on it, lose a turn.*
- *First player to get three in a row wins that game.*
- *Play 3 games. Player winning 2 out of 3 games wins.*

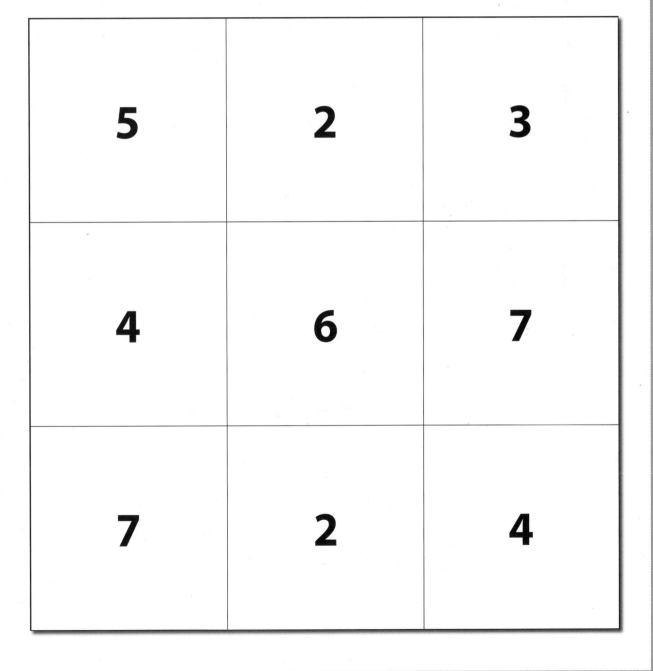

5	2	3
4	6	7
7	2	4

Die Plus Two Tic-Tac-Toe

- Each player chooses a color token (tiles, cubes, chips).
- Players each toss die. Highest number goes first.

How to Play

- *Toss die.*
- *Add two to the number of dots on the die.*
- *Player finds the new number on the grid and places a token on it.*
- *If number has a token on it, lose a turn.*
- *First player to get three in a row wins that game.*
- *Play 3 games. Player winning 2 out of 3 games wins.*

5	**8**	**3**
4	**6**	**7**
7	**8**	**4**

Die Plus Ten Tic-Tac-Toe

- Each player chooses a color token (tiles, cubes, chips).
- Players each toss die. Highest number goes first.

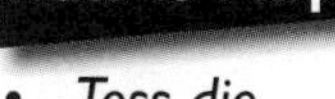

- *Toss die.*
- *Add ten to the number of dots on the die.*
- *Player finds the new number on the grid and places a token on it.*
- *If number has a token on it, lose a turn.*
- *First player to get three in a row wins that game.*
- *Play 3 games. Player winning 2 out of 3 games wins.*

12	**16**	**13**
14	**15**	**14**
11	**13**	**12**

Double the Die Tic-Tac-Toe

- Each player chooses a color token (tiles, cubes, chips).
- Players each toss die. Highest number goes first.

How to Play

- *Toss die.*
- *Double the number of dots on the die.*
- *Player finds the new number on the grid and places a token on it.*
- *If number has a token on it, lose a turn.*
- *First player to get three in a row wins that game.*
- *Play 3 games. Player winning 2 out of 3 games wins.*

10	**2**	**12**
6	**4**	**8**
10	**8**	**6**

Die Plus One and Double Tic-Tac-Toe

- Each player chooses a color token (tiles, cubes, chips).
- Players each toss die. Highest number goes first.

- *Toss die.*
- *Add one to the number of dots on the die and then double the new number.*
- *Player finds the new number on the grid and places a token on it.*
- *If number has a token on it, lose a turn.*
- *First player to get three in a row wins that game.*
- *Play 3 games. Player winning 2 out of 3 games wins.*

10	**4**	**14**
8	**6**	**8**
12	**4**	**10**

Double the Die Plus One Tic-Tac-Toe

- Each player chooses a color token (tiles, cubes, chips).
- Players each toss die. Highest number goes first.

How to Play

- *Toss die.*
- *Double the number of dots on the die and add one.*
- *Player finds the new number on the grid and places a token on it.*
- *If number has a token on it, lose a turn.*
- *First player to get three in a row wins that game.*
- *Play 3 games. Player winning 2 out of 3 games wins.*

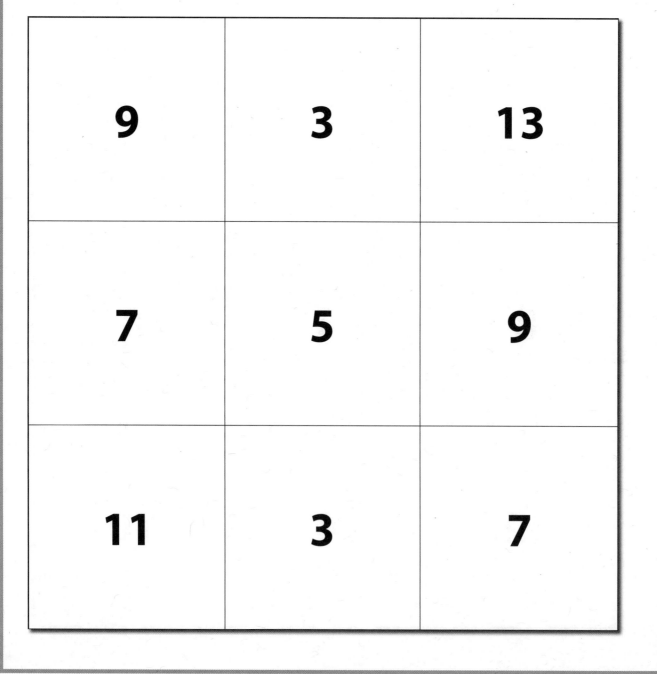

9	3	13
7	5	9
11	3	7

Double the Die Minus One Tic-Tac-Toe

- Each player chooses a color token (tiles, cubes, chips).
- Players each toss die. Highest number goes first.

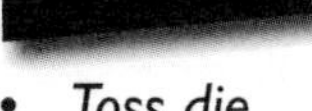

- *Toss die.*
- *Double the number of dots on the die and subtract one.*
- *Player finds the new number on the grid and places a token on it.*
- *If number has a token on it, lose a turn.*
- *First player to get three in a row wins that game.*
- *Play 3 games. Player winning 2 out of 3 games wins.*

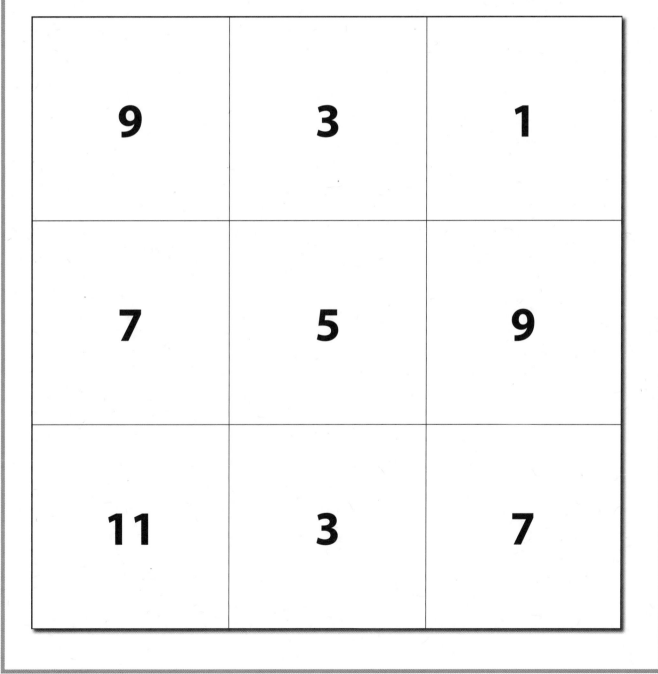

9	3	1
7	5	9
11	3	7

Half-Die Tic-Tac-Toe

- Each player chooses a color token (tiles, cubes, chips).
- Players each toss die. Highest number goes first.

How to Play

- *Toss die.*
- *Find one-half of the number of dots on the die.*
- *Player finds the new number on the grid and places a token on it.*
- *If number has a token on it, lose a turn.*
- *First player to get three in a row wins that game.*
- *Play 3 games. Player winning 2 out of 3 games wins.*

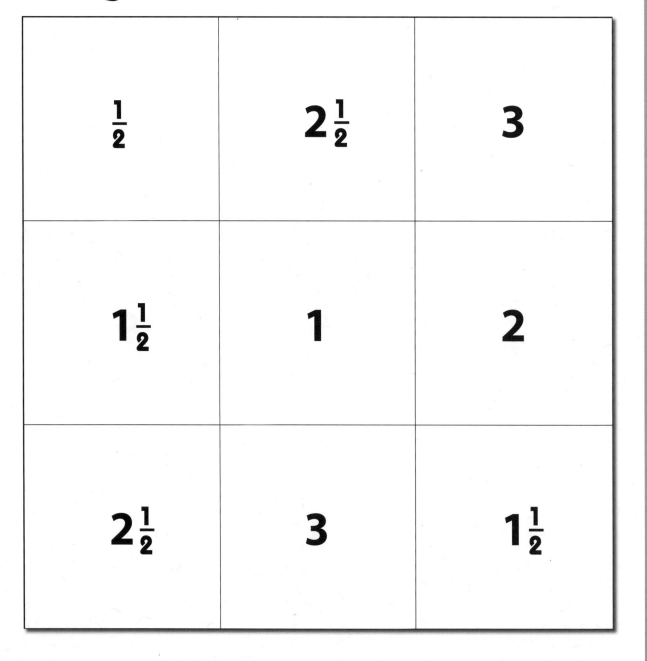

$\frac{1}{2}$	$2\frac{1}{2}$	3
$1\frac{1}{2}$	1	2
$2\frac{1}{2}$	3	$1\frac{1}{2}$

Half-Die 4-Grid Tic-Tac-Toe

- Each player chooses a color token (tiles, cubes, chips).
- Players each toss die. Highest number goes first.

How to Play

- *Toss a die and find one-half of number of the dots on the die.*
- *Player finds the new number on any of the Tic-Tac-Toe grids and places a token on it.*
- *If number is not available on any grid, lose a turn.*
- *When no more winning plays are possible on any of the grids, players count their scores to find the winner.*

$2\frac{1}{2}$	3	1	$1\frac{1}{2}$	2	$2\frac{1}{2}$
$\frac{1}{2}$	$2\frac{1}{2}$	2	3	1	1
$\frac{1}{2}$	$1\frac{1}{2}$	3	2	$\frac{1}{2}$	$2\frac{1}{2}$
1	$\frac{1}{2}$	3	$1\frac{1}{2}$	3	$\frac{1}{2}$
$\frac{1}{2}$	$2\frac{1}{2}$	1	3	2	1
$1\frac{1}{2}$	2	1	$2\frac{1}{2}$	1	2

- Each player chooses a color token (tiles, cubes, chips).
- Players each toss die. Highest number goes first.

Half of Two-Dice Tic-Tac-Toe

How to Play

- *Toss 2 dice.*
- *Find one-half of the sum of the dots on the dice.*
- *Player finds the new number on the grid and places a token on it.*
- *If number has a token on it, lose a turn.*
- *First player to get three in a row wins that game.*
- *Play 3 games. Player winning 2 out of 3 games wins.*

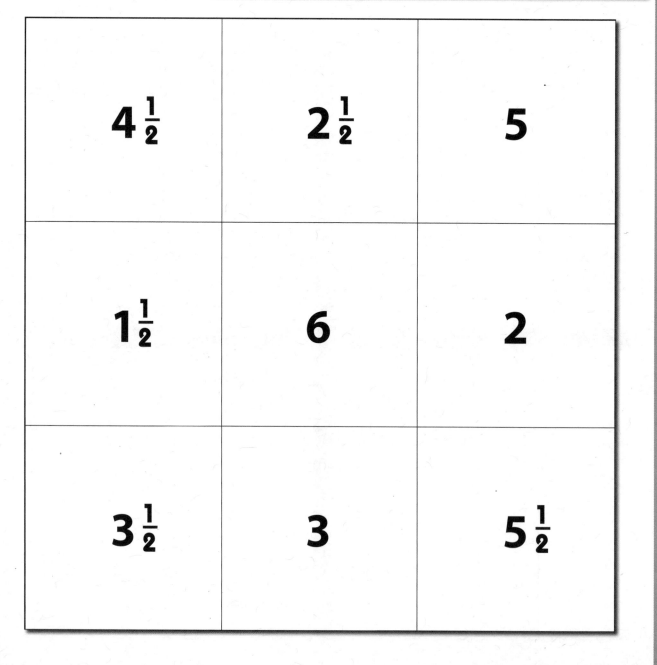

$4\frac{1}{2}$	$2\frac{1}{2}$	5
$1\frac{1}{2}$	6	2
$3\frac{1}{2}$	3	$5\frac{1}{2}$

Half of Two-Dice 4-Grid Tic-Tac-Toe

- Each player chooses a color token (tiles, cubes, chips).
- Players each toss die. Highest number goes first.

How to Play

- *Toss 2 dice and find one-half of the sum of the dots on the dice.*
- *Player finds the new number on any of the grids and places a token on it.*
- *If number is not available on any grid, lose a turn.*
- *When no more winning plays are possible, players count their scores to find the winner.*

$2\frac{1}{2}$	3	5	$1\frac{1}{2}$	4	4
$5\frac{1}{2}$	$4\frac{1}{2}$	6	$3\frac{1}{2}$	3	5
$3\frac{1}{2}$	1	4	2	$4\frac{1}{2}$	$2\frac{1}{2}$
4	5	3	$4\frac{1}{2}$	$3\frac{1}{2}$	$5\frac{1}{2}$
$3\frac{1}{2}$	$2\frac{1}{2}$	$1\frac{1}{2}$	2	4	3
$4\frac{1}{2}$	2	3	$2\frac{1}{2}$	6	$3\frac{1}{2}$

Half of Three-Dice Tic-Tac-Toe

- Each player chooses a color token (tiles, cubes, chips).
- Players each toss die. Highest number goes first.

How to Play

- *Toss 3 dice.*
- *Find one-half of the sum of the dots on the dice.*
- *Player finds the new number on the grid and places a token on it.*
- *If number has a token on it, lose a turn.*
- *First player to get three in a row wins that game.*
- *Play 3 games. Player winning 2 out of 3 games wins.*

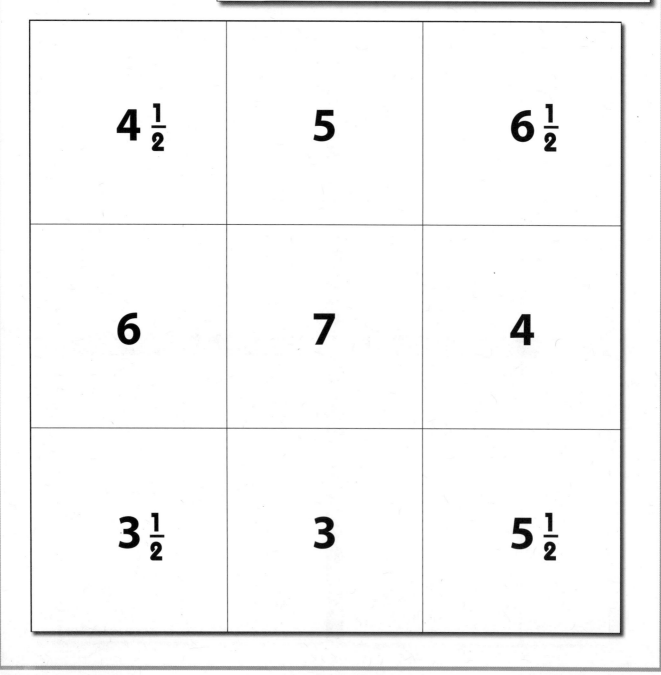

$4\frac{1}{2}$	5	$6\frac{1}{2}$
6	7	4
$3\frac{1}{2}$	3	$5\frac{1}{2}$

Half of Three-Dice 4-Grid Tic-Tac-Toe

- Each player chooses a color token (tiles, cubes, chips).
- Players each toss die. Highest number goes first.

How to Play

- *Toss 3 dice and find one-half of the sum of the dots on the dice.*
- *Player finds the new number on any of the grids and places a token on it.*
- *If number is not available on any grid, lose a turn.*
- *When no more winning plays are possible, players count their scores to find the winner.*

$2\frac{1}{2}$	6	$5\frac{1}{2}$	$1\frac{1}{2}$	3	6
7	4	3	5	$5\frac{1}{2}$	4
6	4	5	9	$6\frac{1}{2}$	$3\frac{1}{2}$
6	4	8	$7\frac{1}{2}$	5	$5\frac{1}{2}$
7	5	$4\frac{1}{2}$	4	6	$4\frac{1}{2}$
$6\frac{1}{2}$	$5\frac{1}{2}$	$3\frac{1}{2}$	$5\frac{1}{2}$	2	$8\frac{1}{2}$

Two-Dice Addition Tic-Tac-Toe

- Each player chooses a color token (tiles, cubes, chips).
- Players each toss die. Highest number goes first.

How to Play

- *Toss 2 dice.*
- *Add the number of dots on the dice.*
- *Player finds the sum on the grid and places a token on it.*
- *If number has a token on it, lose a turn.*
- *First player to get three in a row wins that game.*
- *Play 3 games. Player winning 2 out of 3 games wins.*

10	**4**	**11**
9	**6**	**8**
12	**5**	**7**

Two-Dice Subtraction Tic-Tac-Toe

- Each player chooses a color token (tiles, cubes, chips).
- Players each toss die. Highest number goes first.

How to Play

- *Toss 2 dice.*
- *Subtract smaller number from larger number.*
- *Player finds the difference on the grid and places a token on it.*
- *If number has a token on it, lose a turn.*
- *First player to get three in a row wins that game.*
- *Play 3 games. Player winning 2 out of 3 games wins.*

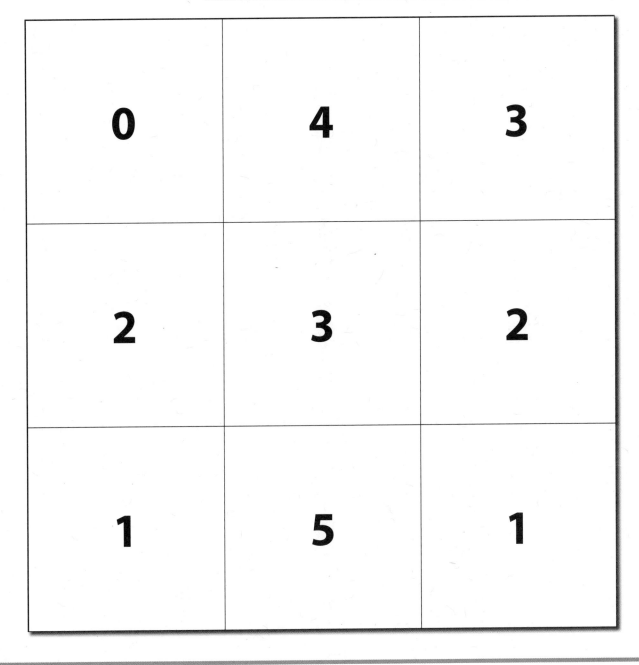

0	**4**	**3**
2	**3**	**2**
1	**5**	**1**

Two-Dice 4-Grid Tic-Tac-Toe

- Each player chooses a color token (tiles, cubes, chips).
- Players each toss die. Highest number goes first.

How to Play

- *Toss 2 dice and add the numbers on the dice.*
- *Player finds the sum on any of the grids and places a token on it.*
- *If number is not available on any grid, lose a turn.*
- *If player tosses three ones or three sixes, toss again.*
- *When no more winning plays are possible on any of the grids, players count their scores to find the winner.*

9	2	8	7	5	4
5	6	7	11	9	6
7	10	8	6	3	8
5	6	10	9	12	10
9	7	4	3	8	5
8	11	9	6	4	7

Two Dice Plus Ten 4-Grid Tic-Tac-Toe

- Each player chooses a color token (tiles, cubes, chips).
- Players each toss die. Highest number goes first.

How to Play

- *Toss 2 dice, find the sum, and add ten to the sum.*
- *Player finds the sum on any of the grids and places a token on it.*
- *If number is not available on any grid, lose a turn.*
- *If player tosses two ones or two sixes, toss again.*
- *When no more winning plays are possible, players count their scores to find the winner.*

14	17	16
18	15	18
15	20	17

18	21	17
17	16	13
19	20	18

18	13	18
19	17	16
17	16	19

16	14	15
15	18	21
17	20	16

Three-Dice 4-Grid Tic-Tac-Toe

- Each player chooses a color token (tiles, cubes, chips).
- Players each toss die. Highest number goes first.

How to Play

- *Toss 3 dice and add the numbers on the dice.*
- *Player finds the sum on any of the grids and places a token on it.*
- *If number is not available on any grid, lose a turn.*
- *If player tosses three ones or three sixes, toss again.*
- *When no more winning plays are possible, players count their scores to find the winner.*

11	12	15	9	12	8
14	10	11	16	11	13
13	14	7	10	5	17
10	4	12	9	15	16
11	9	10	8	13	12
6	11	15	12	11	10

Create Your Own Tic-Tac-Toe

Create a Tic-Tac-Toe activity with your partner.

How to Play

- *Partners agree on the rules for the new activity (for example, toss die, add three).*
- *Figure out which numbers will work for the activity.*
- *Place the numbers on the grid.*
- *Play the activity to make sure it works.*
- *Share it with classmates.*

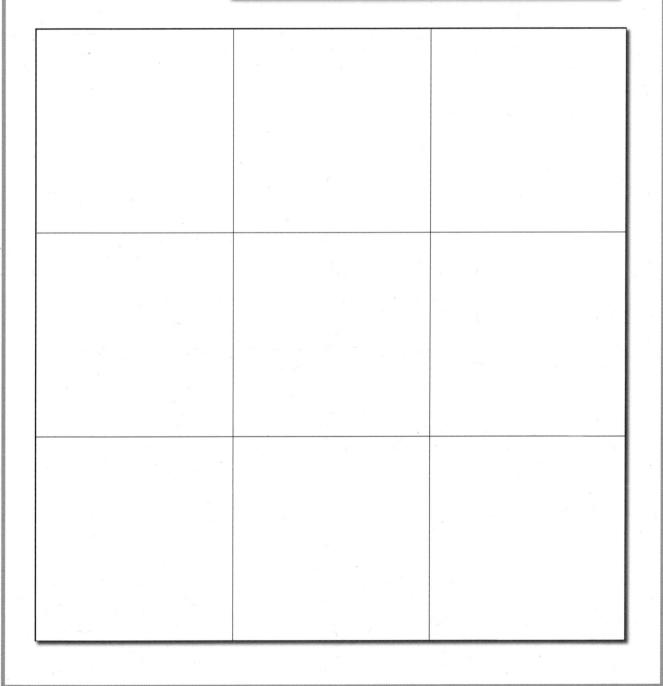

Create Your Own 4-Grid Tic-Tac-Toe

Create a Tic-Tac-Toe activity with your partner.

How to Play

- *Partners agree on the rules for the new activity (for example, toss die, add three).*
- *Figure out which numbers will work for the activity.*
- *Place the numbers on the grid.*
- *Play the activity to make sure it works.*
- *Share it with classmates.*

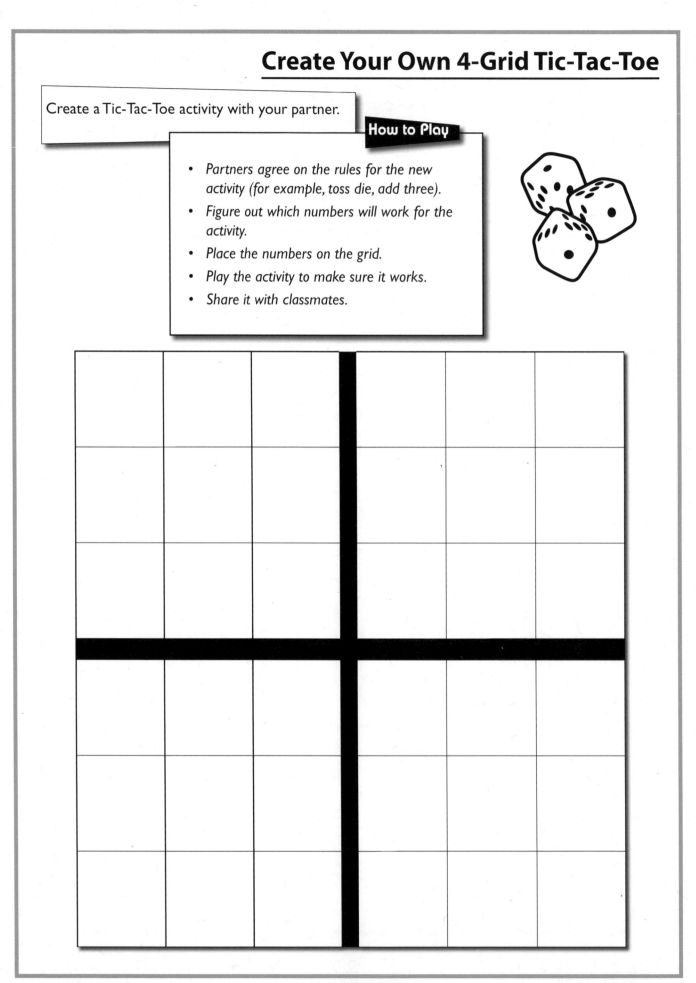

Score Sheet

Directions

- *Choose any of the dice activities.*
- *Toss die. Highest number goes first.*
- *Round 1: Toss die. Perform computation.*
- *Write answer in column for that toss.*
- *After 3 tosses, total the amount.*
- *Round 2: Continue the same dice activity or begin a new one.*
- *After 3 rounds, find the grand total.*
- *Highest total wins.*

Player 1				
	Toss 1	Toss 2	Toss 3	Total
Round 1				
Round 2				
Round 3				
Activity used:			Grand Total =	

Player 2				
	Toss 1	Toss 2	Toss 3	Total
Round 1				
Round 2				
Round 3				
Activity used:			Grand Total =	

About the Authors

The Math of Course group members met while teaching at the Josiah Haynes Elementary School in Sudbury, Massachusetts. They continue their journey together as staff developers in public school districts throughout New England.

Chet Delani holds a doctorate from Boston College and a master's degree in mathematics education from Boston University. A nationally recognized trainer of teachers in grades K–8 mathematics, he is currently on the faculty of Cambridge College, Cambridge, Massachusetts. His work with classroom teachers is supported by 39 years as a classroom teacher and elementary school principal.

Marcia Roak Fitzgerald received a B.A. in elementary education from the University of Maine. During her 30 years as a classroom teacher at the Haynes School, she has used a multimanipulative approach to teaching math.

Karen Kane Moore holds an M.S. in early childhood education from Wheelock College. She is the founder of MathYes, an after-school math enrichment program.

Diane Phelps Neison earned an M.Ed. from Lesley University (formerly Lesley College) and a B.A. in English from Rider University (Lawrenceville, New Jersey). She began her teaching career in New York and New Jersey schools, and has taught at the Haynes School for 26 years.

Mary Holt Saltus earned a CAS degree in human development from Harvard Graduate School of Education and a master's degree from Wheelock College. As a Peace Corps volunteer, she developed math curricula based on a Piagetian model and was involved in teacher training for the Van Leer Foundation for Early Childhood Education. Currently she is researching the links between understanding math concepts and reading comprehension.

The Math of Course group would like to acknowledge their amazing colleague Marge Thurber, who was an early contributor to the development of the dice activities that form this book.